SOLACE

SOLACE

SHULAMITH CHERNOFF

Five Oaks Press
FIVE-OAKS-PRESS.COM

Five Oaks Press
Newburgh, NY 12550
five-oaks-press.com
editor@five-oaks-press.com

ISBN: 978-1-944355-22-7

Cover Art: Raphael Soyer

Cover & Book Design: Lynn Houston

Printed in the United States of America

ACKNOWLEDGMENTS

Some of these poems were included in a collection called *The Stones Bear Witness*, published in 2006 by Hanover Press. Grateful acknowledgement is also made to the editors of the journals in which the following poems first appeared:

Tony Fusco, editor of *Caduceus*: "Breaking the Silence," "Ode to Dreams," and "The Japanese Cherry Tree"

Vivian Shipley, editor of *The Connecticut Review:* "In Fantasy Run Free" and "Gulls Nesting"

Jack Bedell, editor of *Louisiana Literature*: "The Baking Lesson" and "Not Like Other Mothers"

Roderick Bates, editor of *Love & Ensuing Madness*: "Missing"

Corey Cook, editor of *Red Eft Review*: "What Remains" and "Last Passage"

My deepest thanks to the following people:

To Vivian Shipley, who was my guide to the wide world of poetry and who urged me to put together my first book of poems. I am forever grateful to her.

To Lynn Houston, editor of Five Oaks Press, for her sensitivity, patience, and judgment.

To Colette Inez, for her beautiful poetry and wisdom

To Ted Koozer, Stanley Kunitz, and Tuvia Ruebner, whose poems inspire me.

To Carolyn Forche, a great teacher in the summer writing program at Skidmore College

CONTENTS

IV: The River of Names

To my late husband, Dr. Hyman Chernoff

And to my beloved children: Deborah, David, Jonathan, Daniel, Joshua, and Naomi, who died December 30th, 2008

I: The Road Most Traveled

The Road Most Traveled

The road narrows, hidden in fog.
Where great oaks have long since fallen,
saplings grow in their shadows.
My steps slow to the rhythm
of my heart. See how shadows follow me,
call me by my childhood name, Shulenku.
Here is mother Shoshanna, quick of movement
and temper. Scholar father Zvi, whose face
is mirrored in mine. My solemn brother Ben,
pale as alabaster, forever reading in his cloistered room.
This long column of friends, hidden in the graveyard,
whisper of troubled night in my dreams.
Fog obscures this narrowing road, yet I wish
to walk to the very end in jubilation,
not in mounting fear.
Oh governing fates, I implore you—let me
travel on this road a few more years,
for I have miles to go.

Flight

Oh to fly with eagle's wings, rise
toward the warming sun.
Surrender to the shafts of wind,
drift on cumulous clouds
far from the killing fields,
far from the staccato bursts of guns.
To be free, floating above
the savagery of earth.
Before the long night begins,
let me fly. Let me fly.

Follow the Flight of Birds

If, on an early Sunday morning, you decide
to walk down Captain Thomas Boulevard,
in West Haven, Connecticut,
and if you keep to the path
that hugs the shore,
you might spot a woman sitting
on a park bench looking
at the undulation of waves.
She has a book of poetrt in her hand
and is thinking about Ted Koozer, who writes:
Some lonely old man, you thought:
come here to pity himself
in the reliable sadness of grass among graves
but that was not so.

She has come here in early April
when turbulent winds have calmed.
After church, the older Italian men
will come to the bocce courts and women
and children will gather at picnic tables.
Families will picnic under the shade
of trees. All of this brings her comfort:
the promise of spring when
kites begin to soar in the breeze
and dogs on leashes
lead their owners to
confide in one another.

If you think she is lonely,
you are mistaken.
The air is fragrant and the benches,
marked with the names of the dead,
are freshly painted.
She is aware that she has reached
the age of eighty-five without fear.

She can still conjure up poems
in her head and read many books.
This is the way of some old people,
to be content, to remember their
childhood, to make friends
with poets and visionaries,
to follow the flight of birds.

Movement in Slow Motion: Tai Chi

We are learning Tai Chi,
moving slowly to the left,
and then to the right,
stretching arms out,
like seagulls dipping wings,
riding a shaft of wind
in tribute to sun and sky.

I remember the men and women
in Beijing, the ancient ritual
of Tai Chi in Beihai Park, far
from Tian'anmen Square,
where blood stains of dying
students have been erased.
The old people are moving,
eyes shuttered, as if in a trance,
no sign of struggle or surrender.

When we have lived long
and our lives begin to unravel,
we move in languid motion
to bury our fear of collapse.
We learn Tai Chi, the slow
motion of ancient masters.
We reach for sun and sky.

The Solace of Melancholy

It is this hour, this absence of light,
when the black shawl of night
embraces the street, and small
stars of light flicker from windows.
It is the hour of sweet melancholy
when shadowy figures slip away
from the dark. Father and mother
at an open window, calling me home.
School friends whisper of unrequited love,
fierce discussions on New York subways.
It is my hour of solace and melancholy,
holding hands with the ghosts
of a vanished childhood.
Dreams that float through darkened
rooms, visions of another world.

Letter to a Friend

To Elinor, 1921–2007

Is it too much to ask
that you linger
a few more months?
I recall eighty years
of unearthing
our buried lives,
two children on the shore
of Brighton beach gathering
shells in our baskets.
You were the queen of
a mythic tropical island,
a surround of orchids
and tall young men
with piercing eyes,
I, your chief advisor,
sheltered secrets even
our vigilant mothers
could not unearth.

Isn't it too soon
to relinquish your books?
Disclose again
the sexual references
of Aristophanes.
I promise to ply you
with Talmudic interpretations
of Abraham's willingness
to sacrifice Isaac.

Hours communing
with our pianos, teachers
correcting hand positions.
My thundering rendition of
Chopin's revolutionary étude,

Your calm order
of Bach partitas.

The secrets we share
are what I cannot relinquish.
Remember the painters
and musicians
we dallied with,
far from the eyes
of our fierce mothers.

Please linger
at least until
the promise
of spring, when the
lilacs that perfumed
our childhood
bloom again.

Cultivation

To Amoz, who cultivates prize dahlias

The dahlias you have chosen—
their brilliant flowers named
for the botanist Anders Dahl,
bulbs, hidden like jewels,
safe from winter winds,
until the ritual of planting
in the warm breath of spring.

Dahlia is the woman who
drew you to her delicately
with a spread of brilliant petals.
You protect her from winter winds,
prepare her for the blooming.

Not the large-cupped narcissus
for you with white soft petals
and dark orange center,
nor the wind flower anemone's pink
blush and bright yellow eye,
nor the vampire chrysanthemum
on fire blood red.

You are not drawn to the frilly narcissus
nor to *tulipa Angelique*, ruffled in pale rose,
nor do you succumb to the spikes
of *Hyacinthus* perfuming the air.

Dahlias are what you love,
even now in your eightieth year
as you coax them to bloom.
Like your children, they rise
to flower, bending not to your will
but to your patient hands.

The Cormorants of August

Every August I see them
as the early morning sun dapples
the iridescent waters.
Light shafts the moss-covered rock
that juts above the rising tide.
Seven cormorants sit single file,
feathered grey brown
with blue tinged throat pouches,
curving bills. Eyes facing west
in silence, stirring now and then,
a spread and flapping of wings,
like elders on sagging park benches
their memories shuttered
behind a clouded lens.

My father once sat at the window
facing these emerald waters,
contemplating death as he
refused dialysis. Despite my pleas,
he sat in silence, peering at the ocean.
My mother stopped eating, her once
sturdy frame reduced to eighty
pounds, her commanding
voice reduced to a whisper.

I swim nearer, the cormorants
do not move. Sombrous
clouds slowly descend.
A spasm of silence
before the storm.

Crematorium

The ovens, cold, have stopped
their burning. Ashes sifted,
fragmented bone turned under earth.

Poppies wither in the sandy soil.
Grasses burn in the relentless sun.
Oak trees, silent sentinels,
long for a cleansing rain.

No trace of those selected to die.
Fields plowed, barracks lie still
for tourists to hear the silences.

The Cane Bearers

I have finally joined the army of the cane bearers.
Hear our rhythmic tap tap tapping on the sidewalk.
We are aware of our infirmities, balancing our weight,
glancing at the color and shape of our canes.
Mine is silver like the skin of a snake.
Others are paisley, brilliant red and blue, with a few
carved silver handles for the aristocratic bearers.
Armed with my handicap sign, I slide in and out of my car
as kindly shoppers at Stop & Shop help me
with my bundles. I remember ski slopes
and hiking trips in Glacier National Park.
Who is this elderly woman in the army of veterans
with broken limbs, the one who still dreams
of Tuscany and grace like a Ballinese dancer?

A Confession

I have recently acquired the art
of forgetfulness. My sturdy cane
often disappears. Unsteady on my feet,
I keep another on the stairs, happy
to be guided by some divine hand.
And where is my cell phone?
I call from my landline,
Where are you my little one?
I wait for the faint ringing
that leads me to the sofa.
Where, oh where, are my glasses?
They have drifted from the table
to the bathroom. Why did I forget
the last name of my son's second wife?

Here I am at 2 a.m. when a poem
drifted in the still night air and I rushed
to my desk to put words to paper.
Where, oh where, has the brilliant ending flown?
So this is the age of forgetfulness, devoted
to the past, unsure of the present.
Have I forgotten why I wrote this poem?

Poetry Class

Ten women seated around
a dining room table, sharing poems
by Stanley Kunitz, Ted Kooser,
Adrienne Rich, and Natasha Trethewey.
Their words reverberate in our ears,
revelations and voices mingle
with our own. The emptied closets of death,
lilacs that bloom like birthday candles,
each year the solace of solitude.
We have lived with the scent of spring,
endured the winds of winter
warmed by love, melancholic with loss.
Yet here we sit, consumed by the voices
of poets whose words break the still
of the afternoon, stirring memories we share,
seated around this scarred wooden table.

Treadmill

Eighty years old and I am
on the treadmill again.
Five miles now on the road
to nowhere. The television blares
in the gym, a collapse of barracks
in Nasiriyah, a truck bomb explosion,
young soldiers in the rubble.

Walking an endless sloping belt,
memories in the flotsam, debris
of an underground stream.
Here a blaze of ochre, crimson, violet
on the crest of Mt. Sinai, where I once
hiked into a blaze of sun,
into Benedetto's studio, where I posed—
seventeen, naked and proud,
untouchable. The sketches now
hidden from my children's eyes.

Near me in the gym, my friend
Richard lifts weights again.
Forty-two and inconsolable
even though his muscles
bulge and glisten. He groans
under the massive weight.
Young women in spandex,
a display of buttocks and breasts,
the seniors, hesitant and pale,
sag under the weight of age,
step slowly on the moving belt.

Stanley Kunitz's voice in my ear:
The longing for the dance
stirs in the buried life,
One season only, and it's done.

On the treadmill, I am
delaying the season,
the heat still rising
in the buried life.

Creating Poems

The keening of crickets, an evening chorus
in lament of late summer's waning.

The violent bloom of a cherry tree,
incarnadine in spring before the withering.

The roiling waters of the celadon sea
crest in fury then recede to calm.

A shaft of sunlight on the prison floor.
A crocus emerging from a crevice in stone.

Words that erupt in an outburst of journey.
The poet stumbling in the stygian dark.

Poems strewn like stones in a graveyard.
Mourners keening the metaphor.

II: Autobiographia

Autobiographia

In the style of Frank O'Hara's "Autobiographia Literaria"

When I was a child of ten, I was burdened
with gangling arms and legs.
Tall for my age, like my Russian grandfather
who sold grain, fur hats, and boots
to the Cossacks in the Russian town
of Dunayevtza, I liked to linger
in my father's library reading books
that lined the shelves—Freud,
Dostoyevsky, and Bashevis Singer.
Then came a day when my only brother, Ben,
with existential logic, proved to me
that I didn't exist, which made me cry
at unexpected times. Yet here I am,
a mother of six, a professor of education,
widowed and orphaned, yet very much alive.
Oh philosopher brother of mine,
I do exist. I am still here.
I am still here.

Day of Atonement

I see the last light of day flickering
as the congregation, wrapped in prayer
and melancholy, rises to chant seven times:
Adonai hu ha'elohim
The ram's horn is lifted.
Long blasts shatter the silence:
TEKIAH GEDOLAH.

We are in Beth El Synagogue
in Sheepshead Bay, a small wooden building
dwarfed by St. Mary's Church.
I sit in the balcony with my mother,
clutching her skirt. She is pale
as marble, dressed in white silk,
her black braids crisscrossed
like a tiara. The men below
rock back and forth, chanting.

Let us enter your gates at last.

My grandmother Esther prayed in her small
Polish synagogue with my mother
and her five siblings. They fasted all day
until the shofar broke the silence
and night cloaked the town of Tarnov.

Oh God, we beseech you,
grant us atonement.

My towering Russian grandfather, Isaac,
prayed in the town of Dunayevtsa

on Yom Kippur, his five sons swaying
with their father, remembering
the Russian pogroms.

> *L'shana hab-ba-a beyerushalayim.*
> *Next year in Jerusalem.*

The Ethiopian Falashas, in their white robes,
open the ark. Inside the Torahs recline
under the weight of their silver crowns.
The men's ebony hands around the shofar,
Tekiah Gedolah, the long blasts of the ram's horn
as night falls in Addis Ababa.

The Dinosaurs

Torn by dreams. . .
and by the fear that defeats and dreams are one.
—Wallace Stevens

With the lights out,
a sickle moon
casts a shadow on
four-year-old Alexander.
He cowers under blankets
waiting for the roaring,
the razor-sharp teeth.
Stegosaurus looms over him—
two tons and a tail
of bony sharp spikes.
And at the head of the bed
stands Tyrannosaurus Rex
with serrated teeth, ready
to cut through human flesh.

Alexander tosses and whimpers.
He fears being eaten alive.
With a piercing cry, he wakes up as
a dinosaur thunders past.
Now the softness of his mother's
arms, the murmur of his father's
voice. The roaring stops.
The dinosaurs are still.
Small and tranquil, they bask
in the morning light.

When we stoop under the weight
of advancing years, who can we turn to
when night falls and dreams envelop us?
Night visions of relatives, their withered
bodies, the parchment faces of friends

with arms outstretched. We long
for someone to comfort us,
to bring us back to morning's light.

Amina

My mother groan'd, my father wept;
Into the dangerous world I leapt,
Helpless, naked, piping loud,
Like a fiend hid in a cloud.
—William Blake, "Infant Sorrow"

Encased in the warmth
of mother's womb,
your fetal heart
beating faster
in anticipation,
rocking and turning,
head downward,
propelled by waves
of contractions.
Your shoulders wedged
in the birth canal.
The quick arc
of the doctor's scalpel
released you.
After your umbilical cord
was severed, your pulsing
cry, you were lifted
and bathed, placed softly
on your mother's breast.
She called out your name
Amina, she who believes
that the world is hers.

Stages of Darkness

When night descends,
she remembers fear—
age four, the plunge
under covers to escape
from winged vampires,
whose bony fingers
reached out to drag her
from bed.

Autumn days fade,
early shadows cloak
the streets. She remembers
her blossoming body,
age thirteen, hurrying home,
afraid of corner saloons,
drunks who lurked
in alleyways.

Soft summer nights,
eighteen years old,
in the grip of the war
to end all wars.
Caresses of young enlisted
men, kisses tinged
with desperation,
last goodbyes.

When the house grows dark
at the end of day,
it echoes another life.
Now a mother, housebound,
diapers in pails,
pots and pans in the sink,
murmur of children's voices
like the lapping of waves
on a rocky shore.

Only the curtain of night
brings relief, wrapped
in her husband's arms.

When night descends
on the campus,
graduate students hurry
to her illumined classroom,
basking in the heat of discussion.
She is like a preacher
casting words to a devoted flock.
Voices rise and swell,
break the evening silence.

When the shroud of night
drapes her shoulders,
she sits alone in the dark,
eighty-years-old, peering
at the aged cherry tree,
its once abundant arms
sloping, skeletal
in the absence of light.

Split Custody

Monday, she knows it is her mother's turn.
Homework, braided bread, hot
from the oven. Practice Suzuki violin,
the rising warmth of her mother's bed.

Tuesday, the stay at her father's place
with Charlene, his latest girlfriend,
whose children roam the rented house.
Her bunk bed placed in the dark back room.

Wednesday, and it is Pop-Tarts for breakfast.
Rush into the Toyota, late for school again.
Goodbye, darlin', Charlene murmurs to the door.
Too late now to fix the broken string on her violin.

Thursday, back at mom's again.
The nine-year-old stares at her mother's
pale ivory face, sees her red rimmed eyes.
A veil of darkness as the winter day lengthens.

Friday, it's with dad again,
he and Charlene kissing in bed.
Gin and cigarettes, nights at the mall.
Just keep quiet, or he might get mad again.

Saturday and Sunday, all over again.
Misery slapped on a Sunday plate.

Street Games

> *Alas, regardless of their doom,*
> *The little victims play,*
> *No sense have they of ills to come,*
> *Nor care beyond today.*
> —Thomas Gray

Towering elm trees arched their arms
over the unpaved Street in Sheepshead Bay
as the days lengthened, the children
on East Twenty-First Street spilled
out of their houses after supper.

They were a band of six children:
Katie, eight, the fisherman's daughter,
ten-year-old Susie and her twelve-year-old
sister Noreen. Nine-year-old, slow-moving
William in the gray house on the corner.
Then there was Robert, seventeen, tall
and cadaverous, who lived with four old women.

She was nine, tall and muscular.
Her favorite game was stoopball.
She would throw the ball hard
against the steps while the others
ran to catch it without a bounce.
They all played handball against
the side of the house using their hands
to power their shots.
Some evenings they shared secrets,
urinating behind the bushes,
the girls wrapping their skirts as shields,
the boys aiming as high as they could.

In the dusk of an April evening,
when the others had gone home,
Robert invited her to his room

to see his model airplanes
suspended from the ceiling.

Suddenly, he held her tightly,
his heated body throbbing.
Don't be afraid, he said, his face
a pale moon, elusive.
In panic, she tore away
from the coil of his arms,
running back down the stairs,
into the silent street.

The arms of the elm trees beckoned.
She saw the silhouette of her parents
in the dining room,
the glow of the familiar lamp
in her bedroom window,
a beacon in the growing dark.

Not Like Other Mothers

> *Daughter am I in my mother's house*
> *But mistress in my own.*
> —Rudyard Kipling "Our Lady of the Snows"

My mother, Shoshanna, wasn't like other mothers
on Brooklyn's East Twenty-First Street.
For one thing, she had a Hebrew name, Shoshanna,
meaning Rose. She didn't stay home to make lunch
or cupcakes for birthday parties. The other mothers
cleaned their houses, swept the front stoops,
gossiped in the evenings, and went to the movies
with their children on Sunday afternoons.

My mother, Shoshanna, knew she was beautiful
and that my father worshiped her. She held her head
high on a long stalk of neck, wrapped her braids
on top of her head, like a queen's tiara. I was too tall
for my age with skinny gangling arms and legs. At twelve,
I was flat as a board with no sign of rounded breasts

My mother made me wear strange lisle English socks,
and ugly size ten brown shoes with laces. The other girls
had Mary Jane shoes and fluffy angora sweaters.
Don't be vain, my mother said, *and don't slump.*
Forget about what other people think.

My mother was very particular about the friends
that I brought home. They had to be serious readers
and devoted students. *We are Jewish*, my mother said.
You have to become a scholar. You must learn
to play the piano like Rubinstein and Paderewski.

In desperation, I snuck out to visit with Betty and Jeanne,
who painted their fingernails red, wore curlers
at night and padded their bras with wads of cotton.

When I went to study music in Maine, my mother
dared me to jump from a rocky ledge in East Blue Hill.
I plunged into the numbing waters. She laughed as I swam
back to the rocky shore. Not like the others, she always walked
ahead of me. A gnarled stick in hand, she commanded
the retreat of barking dogs. Garter snake slithered away
from her while I gathered blueberries on the mountain incline.

Here are the two of us, in the photograph on the mantle.
My mother sits ramrod straight, her head held high.
I sit at her side, pale in her shadow, plotting a revolution.

The Two Roses

Rosalee Harris arrived at our house,
East Twenty-First Street in Brooklyn, every other week
on Friday at eight a.m. Her ebony face,
frayed at the corners like old cloth, edged
with close cropped gray hair.
Brooding amber eyes, deep and round
as glass marbles. She wore a frayed
wool coat, tan housedress, cotton stockings,
battered leather shoes, worn down at the heels.

My mother stayed home from work those Fridays
preparing equipment and food for her arrival.
Armed with a Hoover vacuum cleaner, Rosalee
roared around the house, sometimes gouging the legs
of tables and chairs. She wielded the mop
in a fury. Cursing under her breath, she roared
through the house like a sirocco wind in the Sinai desert.

My mother Rose, called Rozia in Polish
had a tongue like a knife that could cut
an unsuspecting victim into ribbons.
Quiet and subdued when Rosalee came,
she served her hot lunches on her very best china.
Rosalee's husband has deserted her, she said,
and her only daughter is very mean to her.

One day, Rosalee did not appear.
She is sick, my mother said. *I am going to visit her.*
A cloud of steam rose from the big pot
of chicken soup on the stove. She taped the lid down,
wrapped the pot in newspaper and placed it
carefully in her canvas shopping bag.

She then marched to the BMT Subway,
rode to Harlem ,125th Street.

She found the apartment house,
climbed the five flights of stairs
dragging the heavy pot with her.
Men and women peered out of their windows
to see the imperious white lady, a stranger,
walking down their street, pot in hand.

The two women talked for hours,
eating soup on the kitchen table.
Rozia, once a Poor Polish girl collected debts
for her father in Tarnov, worried about her safety
as a Jew. Rosalee, still raging after being abandoned
by her mother and husband, shared my mother's
inner turmoil, her need to make a name
for herself in America.

When she came home at midnight,
my mother was quiet as a midsummer lake.
Rosalee will recover, she said.
We are the two roses, grafted
from the same ancient stock.

Flight from P.S. 129

Father and mother, you never knew
that for two weeks I wandered
from East 21st Street and Avenue Z
to Ocean Parkway every school day
until the truant officer reported me.
The arms of elm trees cast long shadows
over me, stray dogs and cats
followed in my footsteps.
When the school bell rang
at three, I raced home to bring
good news from kindergarten.

Miss O'Donnell always planted herself
in the doorway of P.S. 129.
Her cheeks were mottled, eyes ice blue,
arms crossed over her ample bosom.
The red brick building like a fortress,
high square windows decorated
each season with five finger turkeys,
Indians with headbands, and triangular
Christmas trees.

She bellowed at children who were seconds late,
too untidy, too bold or foreign looking.
I tried to sneak in as quietly as possible,
tiptoeing to the kindergarten room
where Miss Smith stood waiting.
After saluting the flag, we all sang,
off key, *My country 'tis of thee.*

The rumors began in kindergarten.
The children whispered that if you were
ever caught by Miss O'Donnell, you would
be sent to her office and never seen again.
They said that she had a big strap hidden
in her closet. After she beat you, she would kill you

and throw your body down into the cellar.
They said that hundreds of children
had disappeared from kindergarten.

Each day, my heart leaping with fear,
I thanked Jehovah for protecting me
from Miss O'Donnell, the long fall
down the stairs, and death
in the basement of P.S. 129.

The Baking Lesson

I was five when the baking
lessons began. The two sisters,
Tante Nesia and Tante Ida were
my teachers. Nesia had full breasts,
slender legs, and a scent of dried
rose petals. Her husband gave
her diamond earrings, a mink coat
and two soft, pale children.
Tante Ida had flaming red hair,
large blue eyes ringed with
black pencil, and a fiery temper.
She made hats for Lilly Daché.
She had many friends with names
like Philomena, Rozia, and Zosia.
She marched in labor rallies
and sang freedom songs
in Polish and German.

I was twelve when I graduated
to making apple strudel.
First, we kneaded the dough
until it was smooth and elastic.
Then we rolled it out on
a big floured tablecloth.
We stretched the dough
on the backs of our hands
until it was paper thin.
Then came the filling of apples,
cinnamon, and nuts. The dough
was rolled into a cylinder
and placed gently into the
warm oven.

At twelve, I was into serious books
like Thomas Mann's *The Magic Mountain*
and *War and Peace*. Would I marry

a rich man who would bring me
gifts of limoge china and diamond earrings?
No, I would marry a union leader
who could quote Shakespeare and Rilke.
We would make love all Saturday night.
Then I would get up in the early morning sunlight,
prepare my dough, paper thin, fill
it with apples, cinnamon, and nuts,
bake it in the oven to present
my love with the fragrance
of strudel.

III: Missing

Missing

In a field
I am the absence
of the field.
—Mark Strand, "Keeping Things Whole"

In the sundrenched house
I am the presence
of one.
Your oak desk, medical books,
spartan bed all
declare you
missing.

As I wander from room
to room your photographs
begin to darken.
Schubert's song, *Der Wanderer*
parts the air with longing.
The bass voice of Alexander Kipnis
declares you
missing.

I search for words
to describe your absence.
Strands of metaphors
to make me
whole.

Barge Music

In memory of Naomi

A leaden sky, the weeping
rain, a bleak December.
My daughter's descent,
tethered to an oxygen tank.
Hospice, her two young daughters
huddled in the room.

My need for solace.
The subway ride
with cousin David.
The train rumbling over
the Brooklyn bridge.
A steel grey Sunday afternoon.
The ferry landing,
three arching bridges.
A barge rocking in
roiling waters.

The cellist from Israel.
The storm's fury.
Strains of Bach.
Max Bruch's *Kol Nidrei*.
A throbbing of strings,
the longing for redemption.

The last vibrations of bow,
a moment of silence.
The bravos, the bows.
Did you like the concert?,
David asks her.
I will never forget it.
Lo eshkach l'olam.

The return, the subway,
the shroud of night.
The rain, the void,
the silent scream.

Thirty Days of August

In memory of Dr. Hyman Chernoff, 1918–1972

How did it come to pass
that these six children,
huddled together in a tight
circle of fear,
threw handfuls of crumbling
earth upon your coffin?

Did the rabbi's Aramaic *Yisgadal
Veyiskadash* comfort you
and the God of Abraham
give you solace?
Did long nights of sleep
cradle you, or was this
Aramaic tongue a magic
incantation to bring
you back to me,
to your six children
standing here in shocked
silence?

And it came to pass
on the thirty-first day of August,
in torpid summer's heat,
the telephone rang
to break summer's stillness.
A faint voice slowly intoned
your death, and I stood
there alone.

I went to gather the remnants
of your life; wallet, jacket, manuscript
unfinished, letters held by
a fraying string that bound
us together.

Why does this bed still bear
the curve of circling body,
embrace of pillow,
scent of pipe, troubled
sleep that bears you
towards me everywhere?

Gulls Nesting

. . . and not till the wound heals
and the scar disappears
do we begin to discover
where we are. . .
—Henry David Thoreau

I
Pairs of nesting herring gulls
swoop with a whir
of wing, a shrill
chorus warning their
downy young,
wobbling out of the nest,
as our children race
unguarded in the courtyard
of memory.

II
Early morning sun
dapples Block Island,
shafts curve of beach
mottled with stones.
Rosehip bushes ride
the hills, terns
pockmark sand as
they pace the shallows.

III
Lapping of waves
like your heartbeat
ebbing. Memory
fingers the ridge of
a scar.

IV

In August, a blaze of
sun shimmers sand
sparks ocean to lumined azure.
A frieze of men and women
embracing on the
curve of shore.
My wound, sutured,
bursts.

Hands Holding the Void (Invisible Object)

Sculpture by Alberto Giacometti, 1934

Light hovers over
her angular hands holding
the unseen, the void.
Eyes hollow in their sockets,
mouth open in shock,
Narrow bronze legs pinched together,
defiant of penetration.
Her arms are outstretched,
welcoming my grief.

Giacometti, mourning the death
of his father, created a solitary
woman. She was the *ka* of the
Egyptians, the shaded soul
of the dead. When you died,
I held my tongue, hid my grief,
my body impenetrable.
I measured the seasons
of each year without you.

The dead bring no consolation.
Grief, a sharp wall of defense.
But when August thirty-first returns
each year, a blanket of heat
withers the grass on your grave
as I hold the shaded soul
of the dead in my hands.

January

Snow mounts the azalea and rhododendron,
their tight buds swell with coming
Spring. Winter pales the January sky.

Only the scraping of snow plows
at night. A cold wind chills.
I light a memorial candle,
stack the wood, light the kindling.

My body warms in the goose down
quilt. I sink under the weight
of darkness. Drifting to another

shore, where we slept, cradled
in boughs of pine.
Wakened by the white

light of morning, I turn
to the fire, the embers still spark
the gray ashes.

Storm Tossed

Without you, I have
walked the crescent
beach all day.
The bounty of children
you left me
like the shimmer of mica.
Our footprints erased
in the sand.

Here lie mounds of stones,
coal black lignite, some blood red.
inflamed with iron oxide.
An autumn wind churns
the mounting waves,
hurls them out
to sea, abandons
them on curve
of shore.

Only one stone,
shaped like the crescent
of Block Island
warms the palm
of my hand.
Separated from the others,
metamorphic rock,
striated black and grey.

Oh my stone,
we are both
at the edge of
the turbulent ocean,
Alone in this multitude,
storm tossed, shaped
by the waves that
batter us.

A Corridor of Dreams

Soon after the August of your dying
our towering Japanese cherry tree
garlanded each spring
with bursts of crimson blossoms,
began to bend, limbs cracking
with every gust of wind.

There was a time when we could
barely wait for the cool wrappings of night.
The crumbs of supper had been swept
from the wide-plank floor.
The murmur of our children's voices
slowly subsided to silence.
We sank deep in the warm burrow
of bed, our arms and legs coiled
together, even in sleep.

Sometimes you reappear in dreams.
Pale as alabaster, you hover above me
transparent arms outstretched. Your deep
voice reverberates in my ear.

The night corridor lengthens
as I wander in a darkened labyrinth.
You have begun to fade
like an aging sepia photograph
and I am alone, groping in the dark.

My Japanese Cherry Tree

We had lived together
for more than forty years.
Your furrowed trunk
leaned against the roof
as if you wished to meld
your body to this house.

You are fragile now,
branches snap with
each passing wind.
Your bony silhouette
frames the window,
growing dark.

This is our secret pact:
when garlands of crimson
no longer appear in Spring,
and your last branches
brittle with age, break
under the weight
of winter snow,
I will give way, lower
the shades, surrender.

Last Passage

To my mother Shoshanna, 1893–1994

Your skin is stretched taut
on concave bone, worn thin
by ninety-nine years of battle
with wind, sun, and bursts
of joy and rage.
Your arms that commanded
now quiver, your shrill voice
has softened.
The sapphire blue dress
on your thin shoulders,
a shroud of rustling silk.

Your eyes still retain
their cobalt blue, peer through
the veil of memory.
You recall dense
Polish forests, thrusting trees that
pierce clouds and sky.
Your small town Tarnov,
close to Kraków.
You remember the mushrooms
that carpeted the fields
like waxen flowers.
You see the peasants who
plucked feathers from fattened
Polish geese. You feast on berries,
red garlands that cascaded
from baskets of straw.
The peasant market throbbed
with a babble of tongues,
rising in the humid afternoons.

You have not forgotten
the hymn to Kaiser Wilhelm,

or the samovar and feather bed.
Your silver candlesticks
passed from hand to hand.
You remember all the names
of the first-grade children
in the fading leather album.

World War One:
you took a boat of passage,
spent three weeks in steerage
to arrive at Ellis Island.
Deloused and shorn
of given name,
you proclaimed your right
to conquer America.

What Remains

To my mother, Shoshanna, 1893–1994

After all these years without you,
your bed still remains untouched.
The white goose down quilt from Poland
still bears the imprint of your body.
Photographs crowd your dresser—
you and Aba, your head erect,
your black hair a crown of braids.
Imperious, your swan neck
and blue eyes commanded attention
even then.

With a cloud of dust,
I open your old trunk.
Three braids lie neatly coiled
in paper: one black, one gray, one white
Here is the brass Russian samovar,
a wedding gift in 1913.
Here are the letters, the fine script
in Polish, Russian's French, Hebrew,
love letters from my father
when you visited your parents in Tarnov.
I cannot live without you. I long for you.
I am intruding.

I find your notes to me,
a letter of thanks to Shulenku
for her endless devotion.
Is this the same person I feared
as a child? Your steady script
etched in your diary
before your hands trembled
beyond control

You left instructions for me,
how to open the safe.

You carefully typed the letter:
I must face the hard reality
that my days are coming to an end.
My illness made a great splash
among my grandchildren.
I lived in a state
of pleasant estivation.

You looked at me for the last time
as I held your fraying letters, your master's degree,
pictures of your family in Poland,
the Russian samovar gleaming
in the darkened room.

Ode to Dreams

After "Odas Elementares" by Pablo Neruda

Come to me again
dreams that stir, rise
from the gauze curtain
of the nether world.

I sink into the burrow,
the bed we once shared.
You are peering from the window
of a train. I race alongside
calling out your name,
but the train rumbles faster,
wheels grinding in my ears.

Come to me dreams,
with the apple scent of spring.
You come toward me slowly,
transparent arms outstretched.
Embracing me, you dissolve
in mist. A soft wind
flutters the curtains.

Come to me dreams,
carry me back to the one
who has disappeared.
Tell him that I have endured
the dying leaves of autumn,
a glare of winter ice,
fire of summer,
yet another spring.

To Stefan "Complaint V1"

In loving memory of Stefan Wolpe

I hold your tattered manuscript
for piano, "Complaint V1"
inscribed to me.
Flames still smolder
from pages of
rage and pulsing
beat.

I watched you compose
in the barn on Maine's
East Blue Hill.
You struck the piano,
your rasping voice
rising in augmented
leaps, a nervous beat
that echoed from
the Bauhaus, Moscow,
Tel Aviv, your studio
in New York.

At seventeen years, I
was encircled by your arms
that held so many
women in tight embrace.
Your probing mouth
did not conquer for
I could not bear to suffer.
It was your music
that I yearned for,
the notes that soared
above the flicker
of lanterns in the shadows
of the barn on
East Blue Hill.

When tremors shook
your body like
a leaf in gusts
of wind, I could not
bear to come to you.

Your manuscript
still burns in my hand.

IV: The River of Names

Ground Zero

It is the image, over
and over, the towers collapsing
on flickering television screens,
like the children who build
tall thin towers, a delicate balance,
until an angry fist sends
them tumbling
down.

It is the hand-lettered signs,
Have you seen my mother,
father, daughter, friend?
The hours of waiting,
the brooding
silence.

It is the river of names, first
a stream, then rapids,
names bobbing up
and down in the swift
current, drowning out
the cries of the
living.

It is the shroud of silence
that cloaks the ground:
the zero, a void,
gaping wound,
open mouth, silent
scream.

Columbus Day

Pine Ridge Reservation, South Dakota
Home of the Oglala, home of the Sioux,
Home of Crazy Horse and Red Cloud,
Home of the welfare state, broken
whisky bottles, the jagged glass edge
of despair glints in the morning sun.

Columbus Day, recall
the children, first Americans,
torn from their parents' arms,
braids shorn, pride shorn,
denied their native tongue.

This land once guarded
by ancestral spirits lies scorched
and cracked, nameless streets
without bank or post office.
Only the Gospel Fellowship Church
on the dusty, potholed street.

Druze Widow

A visitor from America,
I climb the narrow path
coiling through the Druze village
Daliat el Carmel.
White stucco houses
mount the hills, shimmer
under an unyielding sun.

Samia waits under the arched
doorway. Twenty-three years old,
with three children. Widow
of Khamal Halabi, who stood watch
in Lebanon with Amnon Halevi
when a bomb exploded, killed Khamal,
shattered Amnon's legs.

Samia's face is etched
in stone, her eyes hollow.
This army of our sons and husbands
has left us in grief.
We are all widows, Jews and Arabs.
When will it all end?

I have no answer
as the sun bears down
on undulating hills.
A burst of gunfire
stabs the air.
Young soldiers patrol
the killing fields.

That Butterfly Was the Last One

> For Pavel Friedman, who died June 8, 1944
> in the Terezin concentration camp

> *That butterfly was the last one.*
> *Butterflies don't live here in the*
> *ghetto…*

Sixty kilometers north of Prague
lies Terezin, Emperor Joseph's old
garrison town, narrow in the confluence
of the Vltava and Labe rivers. The Pinkasova
synagogue, built in 1538, bears the names
of seven thousand five hundred children
on its walls. Franz Kafka lived on Zlata Ulicka 22,
where he wrote of his longing to leave
Prague, "the little mother with claws."

> In 1942, Richard Heydrich showed the Red Cross delegates
> his model camp, where fifteen thousand children
> learned to paint, sculpt, write poetry, like Kafka's
> *Metamorphosis*. In 1944, selected transports
> took the children to Auschwitz.

> *Perhaps if the sun's tears would sing*
> *against a white stone…*

Pavel, you were fourteen, the ripe age of my sons
when you came to this place. The sun rose daily
to warm the fifteen thousand children of Terezin.
Golden butterflies swarmed over the distant hills.
Your teacher, Friedel Dicker-Brandeis, brought you paints
and paper, books with the paintings of Vaclav Sparla
and Emil Fila. Then she disappeared in the transport
to Birkenau. You chose to engrave your pain on paper,
your words flowing like the swift Vltava River.

> *The dandelions call to me*
> *and the white chestnut branches in the court.*

Perhaps you wrote your poem here,
near the window, the white chestnut
tree in full bloom. Did you see the other
children roam the streets, the echo of
their laughter in your ear? You must have seen
the blue ribbon of highway leading to Prague.

> How could you know that even as the dandelions
> called to you, and the white chestnut beckoned,
> that you would never see another butterfly?

Crossing Bridges

Dedicated to Mae Gibson Brown, teacher and gospel singer

Her voice soars in the darkened room,
rises over The Salt and Pepper Gospel Singers.
I never could have made it.
Hear the mourning and the melancholy.
A song of field workers,
in the cold of winter and
the sweet fragrance of spring.
Mae Brown, Momma Brown,
arms outstretched, strong
in the wealth of seventy years.

Remember the coal miner's daughter,
a witness to the bone chilling
winters and disasters in the mine.
The child who asked,
Why are there two bridges,
one for blacks and one
for whites? Why can't I try on
clothes in the store?
Why doesn't the school bus
pick me up?
Why, why, why?

Testing the limits, she walked
over the bridge for whites.
What was different on the other side?
Reported by the neighbors,
her parents waiting, the sharp sting
of the strap, fear of another
body floating in the creek.

She never knew hunger,
sustained by Major Gibson's garden.
New dresses sewn from flour sacks.

She never knew she was poor.
Seventy now, she has tested the bridges.
Her voice, rises above the others,
She has crossed to the other side.

Coming Home to Georgetown, South Carolina

In memory of Minnie Kennedy

Ancient oak trees give shade
to the narrow front porch.
326 Queen Street.
Georgetown, South Carolina
Ninety years have etched her face,
her toothless smile wide and welcoming.
This is the house that her parents built,
where oleander perfumes the air
and sparrows sing their
plaintive songs.

Minnie Kennedy, born and raised
on the plantation of financier Bernard Baruch,
Hobcaw Barony, where rich New Yorkers
came to be entertained. When Belle Baruch
asked the black workers to dance
for the amusement of her guests,
Minnie and her mother the cook,
sat in sullen silence. Her docile
father watched their defiance
in dismay.

Here lies Front Street, the two story
pastel houses from the seventeen hundreds.
The waterfront a confluence of five rivers
the Santee, Black. Pee Dee, Waccamaw and Sanye.
Once home to indigo and Louisiana rice
where slaves from Madagascar slogged
through the swamps clearing Cypress
and Tupelo trees.

Note the legacy of the English:
Queen Street, King Street, Bishop Street,
High market and Cannon street.

Minnie has come home after sixty years
of teaching in New York
Here are the antebellum houses,
churches, alcoholics anonymous,
preachers and drinkers.

See the rockers on the front porches,
A portrait of Martin Luther King
in Minnie's living room,
African carvings on the wall.
She has come home to the quiet
of her home town, where history
is forgotten, and the community
slumbers in the summer afternoons.

Tel Aviv, October 2013

Giant cranes hover over city streets
teeming with cars and pedestrians.
New buildings soar towards
a constable sky, azure blue,
drifts of clouds and a warming sun.
Cafes line the streets, tables laden
with pita, hummus, gelato, espresso.

Palm trees line the boulevard,
elders sit on benches, muse
and watch the passing crowds.
Young Israelis, in jeans, t-shirts,
running shoes, cell phones
a third ear. The new plaza
museum, opera house, Habima,
an Israeli Lincoln Center.

The Yarkon river glistens,
beckons from my window,
and yet, anxiety persists.
The left and the right,
rabbis and secularists.
Two armies in conflict.
Arab villages, the check points,
refugees seeking shelter.
Listen while the world waits,
the city soars, blotting
out the name Armegeddon.

Cousin Rivka

The year of Hitler's rage,
Poland's invasion, your battered
suitcase arrived at our door,
cousin Rivka. Your photograph
placed by mine on the mantle.
Fourteen years old and big
for your age. Pale oval face,
almond eyes, thick waist-length braids,
a faint crease of a smile.

You never arrived, cousin Rivka.
Your papers were in order,
affidavits sealed and processed,
and we waited for you. Waited.

If I had been in your place,
evicted from my school
for a star of David on my sleeve,
I would have answered in terror,
when the brownshirts hammered
at the door, clinging to my suitcase,
herded to the station,
the dogs barking at my heels.

If I had been in your place,
I would have been sealed in
a cattle train with the others.
The train would have rumbled
through forests of fragrant pine,
meadows dotted with *stotrotka*.

I would have been silenced by terror
as mother, father, and little Henek
were motioned to the left,
and I was motioned to the right.
They would have taken my braids,

my hair shorn to wiry stubble, clothed
in the prison stripes, while I waited,
waited for a letter of salvation.

Cousin, my cousin,
when the armies came to Auschwitz
and the prisoners stumbled through the gate,
We could never find you.
Were you hidden in the ashes,
the ashes, the ashes?

In Fantasy Run Free

For Mina Pächter and the women who perished in Terezín

Dear Anny,

Remember when we lived in Prague,
lingered over a late breakfast;
déjeuner a la fourchette, sandwich,
sausage, hard boiled eggs.
In 1939, I told you that I could not leave.
You don't move an old tree, I said.
I now find myself in Theriesenstadt,
the spa of privileged resettlement, we were told.
My body has withered from hunger, frozen
by the fierce wind that shudders our barracks.

At night, wrapped in darkness,
we all exchange recipes. I offer
my leberknodel, liver dumplings
with a taste of ginger, and Kletzenbrot,
my rich fruit bread.
Even when my hand trembles,
I know I must finish my Kochbuch.

Cooking with the mouth, we said,
remembering our former lives,
our bodies bone-thin, arguing
over our recipes: the Mikado torte
with caramelized sugar and my Pirogen
rolled with potatoes and chopped cracklings.

While I fought for pale bowls of soup
and stole raw potato skins,
I offered my recipe for vanilla cake
with five egg yolks, vanilla bean, ground hazelnuts
and twenty decagrams of sugar.

Anny, I am wrapping these recipes for you
in this book, handsewn. *Remember my Kochbuch.*
Please petricku, do not forget your babi.
I call the last of my recipes for cake
Lasse der Fantasie freien lauf.
In fantasy run free.
                    Mina

These Are the Stones

I
These are the stones,
the ancient stones
that form the wall
bathed in the light
of Jerusalem.
Here are the men
who rock back and forth,
the women who cover
their sorrow in shawls,
whose prayers are hidden
in chinks in the wall.

II
These are the stones
that lead to the gates
that circle the walls
of Jerusalem.
The Dung Gate,
the shimmer of stones,
the ruins of
King Solomon's Temple.

III
El Aksa Mosque
where Muslims pray
south towards Mecca.
The Lion's Gate
that leads to the
Via Dolorosa.
The stations of the cross
where Jesus walked.
Hadrian's Arch and
the Ecco Homo convent
of the Sisters of Zion.

IV
These are the stones
that bear the carvings

in the courtyard of
Deir es Sultan
where Ethiopian monks
walk in muted prayer.
Here the Jaffa Gate
that harbors the stones
of the old city walls
of the Ottoman Sultan
Suleyman the Magnificent.

V
These are the stones
of Jerusalem's ramparts,
past Zion Gate,
the Domition Abbey,
the invisible lines of all four quarters:
Muslim, Christian
Jewish, Armenian.

VI
These are the stones
thrown by the men
who carry the anger
that brings the tanks
that break the houses
that bring back the stones
that litter the streets
of Jerusalem.

VII
These are the stones
that mark the graves
of those who died
to claim the land.
The Cypress trees
bend in the wind.
These are the stones
that bear witness.

44806655R00061

Made in the USA
Middletown, DE
16 June 2017